# Secrets and Desires of the Heart

© 2012 Kellie Kamryn
ISBN 978-1-935757-59-7

Published by
Romance Divine LLC
www.romancedivine.com

# Dedication

To the "muses" who inspired the pieces—touching my life in some way, and never leaving me the same.

# *From the Author*

My poetry always comes from a very personal place. Not that I everything I experience everything I write about, but rather something in my life will inspire a piece to be written. Like my novel and short story writing, my poetry takes on a life of its own and I never know how it will end until I've finished. The poems in the collection are guaranteed to touch your heart, whether it makes you sad, fills you with love, or titillates your senses. Just as there is a love that makes you feel full to bursting and on top of the world, there is the darker side of love people hope they never encounter. And of course, who could forget how lust plays a part in matters of the heart! A couple of the erotic poems were written to rise to the challenge of other authors who dared me to push the envelope in my writing. Thank you for that.

I'm certain everyone will find at least one piece that will become their favorite. And now I present to you, Secrets and Desires of the Heart…

# SECRETS
## and
# DESIRES
## of
# The Heart

## Kellie Kamryn

# Secrets

# Of

# The

# Heart

# Afterglow

As I rest my head upon your chest
your arm drapes over me, brushing my breast;
I listen as our heartbeats do slow,
our breathing calming in the afterglow…

Slick and moist our skin does cling,
molds us together, and in our wildest imagining
would never have prepared us – oh no,
as we enjoy the return in the afterglow…

Soon I hear you snore as sleep does overtake,
reminiscing on our match, I lie awake,
wishing that years of this for us will it go
as I fall asleep next to you in the afterglow…

# Dark Side of Love

I never knew a good boxer you'd make,
or that I'd have to duck the swings at me you'd take;
although you'd never use your fists to bruise,
your blows would come from the words you'd choose.

For years I stood and took the blows,
why I stayed, God only knows;
I guess underneath it all, I did see
the man inside that you could be.

Your words on me cast much self-doubt,
I'd question myself, going off to think things out,
not realizing this was your goal all along—
to make me feel bad, so you wouldn't be wrong.

You hurt me on purpose, years 'til I understood
it masked the hurt you felt, over yourself like a hood,
and now I no longer fall for your little game,
I don't believe what you say, no longer feel shame.

None of what you say is true!

Never again will I feel blue!

But now I don't know where I stand…

I really need a helping hand.

Do I have the strength to walk away from you?

Or will I self-destruct like you do?

# Seems Like Yesterday

I still feel the pressure of your lips from our first kiss,
sharing late night hot tubs,
surrounded  by new love's heady bliss.
Seems like yesterday, just yesterday...

With a graduation suit, and a little black dress
we went to town,
not knowing one day we'd trade them in
for a tuxedo and wedding gown.
Seems like yesterday, just yesterday...

From dates at the Ex and kissing in the rain,
to riding around on the Tinkertown train.
Seems like yesterday, just yesterday...

Our first born we had, then it turned to two,
three and four,
we thought we had it all, but then gained so much more,
Seems like yesterday, just yesterday...

A one-bedroom place was our first home,
then a tiny house we fixed 'til it shone,
moved on to something bigger with a yard for the kids
never in Vegas could I have won so much with one bid.

Through it all we vowed to stay together,
never to be alone
when I reflect on all that's transpired,
where has the time gone?
Seems like yesterday, just yesterday...

# All I Have to Give

All I have to give is me
it's all you've ever wanted,
when I look into your big brown eyes
my past mistakes leave me haunted.

Diamonds, pearls, and fancy cars
trips for two around the world;
I was too blind to see that
all you wanted was  to be my girl.

You never gave up on our love
when I thought it was over, my die cast;
You managed to keep up with me
even when I ran from the past.

With the bottle and my big, bad ways
my pain I've always tried to hide;
through it all, you never left
you taught me to see the bright side.

You thought I could be so much more
you never let me give up or give in;
now I'm starting to understand
and feel it in my soul within.

All I have to give is me
surrendering my heart to you;
take it my love, I'm begging
down on my knees if I have to.

I swear I'll prove them wrong for
thinking I don't deserve this chance;
always in me you believed
forever, may I have this dance?

I want you for the rest of my life
so wonderful I know it could be
take my hand, you have my heart
and trust in us for eternity.

# Me Missing You, Missing Me

You called me up the other day
when you were on business far away,
fresh from the shower you'd stepped out
and just so happened to look about.

Up popped my face on your computer screen
wearing a smile that before you'd seen,
filling your head with thoughts of me,
making you wish I was there physically.

Little did you realize that just then,
miles away and with discretion
I had thoughts of you in the same fashion,
lust-filled imaginings and burning passion.

Counting down the minutes now
'til your return, I think of how
we'll welcome with arms open wide,
a smile for each other, and no need to hide
the passion we feel for the other,
and lock out the world my wonderful lover!

# And Love Is?

My heart always knew as much—
I can look, but cannot touch;
I watch you from across the room,
feeling only certain gloom.
Emotions I run from, but cannot hide,
butterflies thump 'gainst me inside,
in your ear I want to whisper,
so jealous am I when I see you kiss her.
Wishing that it could be me,
knowing that me you'll never see;

On the perimeter I do hover,
now I see you moving over,
my breath I suddenly intake,
of myself, a fool I don't want to make,
catch your gaze and hold it steady,
with some words, I try to be ready,
my heart is thumping so wildly,
you smile, showing interest mildly.
Wishing to have magical powers,
to keep you here, talking for hours;
She steps by your side, I feel such grief,
our interlude was much too brief.

As you turn and take her hand,
our moment's gone, like wind-blown sand,
knowing I could never be a cheater,
and at this game, I'll never beat her.
The strain in my voice is hard to bear,
I'm hoping that it, you won't hear
as you go, you bid me good-bye,
(hope you don't see the tear in my eye).
Of your life I'll never be a part,
sadness this brings, breaking my heart;
I turn away and scold myself,
this madness is not good for my health!
Surely there must be in the world
someone to think of me as their special girl?
When will I ever find another?
It hurts so much—why even bother?
I find myself wishing on a star,
for someone to love not from afar.
Do I really know what love is
when the one I want won't give me his?

# The Most Beautiful
# Thing I Wear

Painted eyes and glossy lips,
or a beautiful dress that hugs me at the hips.
But the most beautiful thing I wear, you see,
is the arms of my man around me.

High-heeled shoes and a mini-skirt,
a tight fitting tank or a man's T-shirt,
but the most beautiful thing I wear, you see,
is the arms of my man around me.

A little perfume and a black lace bra,
matching undies and he's in awe,
but the most beautiful thing I wear, you see,
is the arms of my man around me.

Strappy sandals and tight blue jeans,
a form-fitting T — you know what I mean!
but the most beautiful thing I wear, you see,
is the arms of my man around me.

A couple of diamonds and the right accessories,
the right shade color of a revealing bikini,
but the most beautiful thing I wear, you see,
is the arms of my man around me.

Lacey, sexy pink see through lingerie
or flannel pajamas — depends on my mood today,
but the most beautiful thing I wear, you see,
is the arms of my man around me.

# Together They Stand

In starry skies rises the full moon,
lovers embrace by the fire and soon,
they will engage in that magical dance
when one's filled with longing, lust and romance.

The wind rustles the leaves overhead,
a blanket by the fire, tonight is their bed,
nature and darkness, they do surround,
unseen eyes known only by the rustling sounds.

These whispers of night are the only witnesses,
to their every kiss and most tender caresses,
smoke lightly blows to blanket them both,
the universe stands watch as they honor their oath.

Many long years they have loved one another,
knowing they have eyes only for the other,
drawn together like moths to a flame
each burning with a desire that carries no shame.
Wanting only each other to love and to cherish,
heeding innermost desires, fulfilling every wish,
clothes are shed and flung about in a flurry,
they then slow their pace as there's no need to hurry.

Every inch do they know, seems like forever,
a familiarity that grows with years together,
only wanting to bring the other pleasure,
these moments alone, they always will treasure.

Now exploring each other as if for the first time,
the promise of ecstasy heightens the climb;
like just ripened fruit, delicious and fresh,
the taste of their skin, the feel of flesh upon flesh.

Like a runaway train that cannot stop,
their passion has filled them up to the top,
everything explodes, soaring beyond what they know,
sailing so high, their return is so slow.

Clinging together, feeling shattered yet whole,
as one, feeling bliss for this moment they stole,
lying together, listening to their hearts beat,
hunger's now fulfilled and all is complete,
fingers entwined, warmth spreads like hot sun on sand,
reaffirming their vow that together they stand.

# In A Dream

I've seen your face in a dream
and I don't know what it means;
all I can do is stop and stare
into your green eyes as you sit there.

I don't know where you came from
but I long for the nights when you come,
I wonder if this is wrong,
but the pull towards you, so damn strong…

Every night when I close my eyes
I wonder if you'll come in disguise,
but it's always you I see,
and you disarm me so easily.

When you take me into your arms
surrounding me with all of your charms,
with you here, I'm content and complete
to love like this is fruit so sweet.

Hold me close — don't let me go.
Do I believe in magic? I don't know.
Your eyes drown me in their sea of green,
I'm lost in you, in the waves unseen…

Your lips are soft as a painter's brush
our quiet, whispered words of love – hushed,
smooth as silk, skin upon skin
paints a perfect picture of our passion.

When I wake, I long for more
dazed and confused, like I've washed up on shore.
Is it possible to have a lover on another plane?
This makes me sound so insane…

The sun rises bringing morning light,
chasing away the shadows of night.
Here in my bed, I'm now so alone,
Oh, my lover, where have you gone?

# First Love

First love — how sweet it is at the start,
giving love from yourself, surrendering your heart;
when first you walk together, entwined hand in hand,
your gaze to each other stops you where you stand.
Butterflies flit furiously
when the other walks in the room,
a tender smile and sweet caress takes away all gloom,
the only thought you have
is when to see each other next,
when plans fall through,
feel as though you've been hexed.
In love everyone else appears so downtrodden,
first love's a first of many things
that are never forgotten.

Going out together, deciding on a place for a first date,
so nervous you both were that a thing you hardly ate
call each other up, staying on the phone for hours,
never tiring of one another,
under a spell of such magical powers,
the first time you dance, holding each other so near,
nothing else exists,
but the faint whispers in each other's ear

desperately planning stolen moments alone,
wanting to be with one another,
no wish to be on your own.

The first embrace of another's arms
enveloping you so tender,
anticipation of loves first kiss, always you'll remember,
the feel of their lips against yours sets you on fire,
so hard to keep your head, fighting hormonal desire;
hands tremble when they brush past your breast
feeling his weight as he draws you to his chest,
always the question of how much of yourself to give,
with yourself in later years,
this decision you have to live.

How crushed you feel when you have the first fight
crying outward or in, can't sleep much at night,
just want to make up, how sorry you are,
pushing issues aside, placing it behind you so far.
so much to learn but you don't really know
how you change as a person, how love makes you grow,
these feelings so real, wish it to last forever
but rarely it does, though could it ever?
Ah, first love – how sweet it is at the start,
How unfortunate it almost always breaks your heart.

# Bliss

With his eyes, he does undress,
a feathery kiss, a tender caress,
he gives me chase, but after a fashion,
he captures, his kisses filling me with passion.
Slowly then the clothes are shed,
he lowers me carefully to the bed,
a hand behind my head he guides,
before beside of me he lies.
Each tender stroke and loving kiss,
brings the most glorious bliss,
he always knows just the right spot
to stir the coals and keep them hot!
He keeps me lingering on the brink,
he knows how to get to me, I think.
Opening myself up to him
with great joy I invite him in,
so much pleasure for us to gain,
consciously never to bring any pain.
Rise and fall, climbing higher still,
striving for the peak of that glorious hill,
'til at last we hold back no longer,
flying together, our love made stronger.

I hold and to him I cling,
such wonderful memories to each other we bring,
even though we are now bone-tired,
awakened in us is our desire.
Holding me as we feign sleep,
your touch, from me you can't keep,
and so we drift into the land of dreams,
where nothing is at all what it seems,
and here again love knows no bounds,
and we continue to seduce for another round,
'til we awake and once more are together,
beginning another interlude with each other.

# Wedding Day

On your wedding day may you never forget,
the way you feel now or when you first met.
I hope you always look into the other's eyes
and see only clear and sunny skies.
People always have so much advice to give,
but only the two of you can choose how to live.
Should you need to navigate stormy weather,
may you always find a way to do it together.
Remember women may change but love her no less,
always gaze upon her like the goddess she is.
There may be times when he "acts like a man",
but remember he's doing the best that he can.
Should children one day your way come,
remember it's okay to leave them at home
with someone who cares just for a while,
so you can spend time making each other smile.

Sometimes in your lives separate paths you may go,
but may you find the way back together and know…
It is necessary to grow and to learn
but staying together has many rewards to earn.
Life really is not a fairy tale,
marriage takes work, but if done you'll not fail,
always remember what love truly is -
two people as one, but still hers and his.

# Unhealthy Love

Even though the lessons were supposed to be joint,
I now know I will always disappoint,
no matter how good I am at being me,
the real me inside you'll never see.
With this knowledge I have to live,
wanting your unconditional love to give,
sometimes it seems there is no other way,
and I have to live with this day after day.

Wanting you to understand and accept
me the way I do for you, but I only get
hurt and a life filled with lies and deceit,
most days I bow and accept my defeat.
No matter what I do, I'll never get it right,
but there are others who understand my plight,
not much they can do to help me get through,
but their ear to lend me refreshes me anew;
wishing some days you'd put on the other shoe
and see me for who I am and the good that I do.

For so long I have only served to please,

used to feel I was begging on my knees.

Finally, some courage I've come to muster

while you stand and to me, more lies you bluster.

Pretending to me that everything is so fine

that it's all in my head, and I should stop my whine.

Then it starts all over again behind my back,

another piece of me you take in the attack.

No more do I play in this sick little game!

No more will I lie here and take the blame!

For I know I am light and truly goodness,

I won't let you take another piece, making me less;

I forgive you again, know you can't help what you do,

living with knowing I can't count on you.

Everyday sending my prayers to heaven above

asking for help with this unhealthy love.

# Keeper of My Heart

So sad and lonely I feel,
these feelings, are hard to deal;
happy to be, know I ought,
it's not anyone's fault,
some days are an uphill climb
when I miss you all the time.

Wishing you were here with me,
at your side I want to be,
most days are better than others
and never could I love another,
wanting to be in your arms
surrounded by your smile and charms.

Find myself wanting you so bad,
you're the best lover I've ever had,
want to feel your warm embrace
and plant my kisses all over your face,
wishing for you to not want to go away,
with me always I want you to stay.

Only temporary is the situation,
trying to improve your life's station,
working so hard you always do,
lucky I fell in love with you,
so much we've been through together,
life is sure to get better and better.

Through rough times and bad,
through happy days and sad,
through thick and through thin,
with you I've always been,
and in the days that are ahead,
we'll sail on in our own stead,
no matter where you go
I always want you to know
that we will never be apart,
keepers we are to each other's heart.

# Connection

Times come upon us when we don't connect,
my heart hurts and I feel so deject,
my soul longs to feel yours reaching for me,
a tender embrace is what I need, you see.

The times your attention goes astray,
I feel lost, you're a million miles away,
even though in bed next to me you lie beside,
it feels as though there's a great divide.

Needing to remember how you love me so,
it's always present, even when it doesn't visibly show,
I hope my needs you don't come to resent,
your love for me is the most wonderful present.

Even though there are times in between,
the fires burn low and it surely seems,
we wonder if we could resurrect the spark,
to light the fire that saves us from the dark.

My head on your chest, I feel your heart beat,
the warmth of your body a delightful treat,
tracing patterns with your fingertips on my skin,
the contact for me awakens within.

The hunger I have to feel your touch,
mind at ease, knowing we love each other so much,
the love we make together is anything but mild,
all the right places to touch, driving each other wild,
just when I'm sure that better it can't get,
you up the ante, forcing me to place my bet.

Continually to new heights we go,
sometimes it is quick, other times so slow;
over the years it has gone beyond measure,
in any comprehensible amount to our pleasure,
when together the summit we reach,
pure paradise found, the tears I shed each
are because I feel we have become one,
my soul embraces yours; this is more than just fun.
You are my partner, equals we are in our life
fortunate we are to be husband and wife.

# Beautiful Lady

Beautiful lady,
I've been thinkin' lately,
you should come away with me
where's so much of the world to see.
Beautiful lady…
Won't you come with me?

Beautiful sunshine,
you know you are so fine,
this is not a pretty line
'cause you know your heart's all mine.
My beautiful sunshine…
Please be mine?

Come and take my hand,
let's go and make our stand,
rough and stormy seas we'll weather,
forever and together,
just come with me.
My beautiful lady…

My heart belongs to you
I'm ready to say "I do"
will you take this chance,
and forever have this dance?
So come with me,
say you'll come with me
my beautiful lady

# Last Place

Didn't think I'd lose the race
and find myself in this place,
how could he walk out the door
telling me he didn't want this anymore?

After all that we've been through
by his side I stayed true,
How can he say he's had enough?
Does he really think I'm that tough?

When he walked, he took my heart
and broke our promise to never be apart,
Was this all something he had planned -
To break his vow to forever hold my hand?

So many times I picked the pieces off the floor,
but he walked out, said he couldn't do it anymore,
Now what the hell am I supposed to do?
Lying here numb, feeling desperately blue…

Everyone tells me to move on
but can I do that when half of me is gone?
Put on a brave face and act strong,
can't keep up this act for too long…

Part of me knows that I'll be fine
(repeat to myself that little rhyme),
remember the good things in my life
I will get through this strife.

Maybe now we can both be free
and seek out our own destiny,
wouldn't it be good to finally laugh
and for once, follow my own path?

I'm going somewhere to start anew,
pick up my heart and self-esteem, too,
can't let this get me down
refuse to let me or the kids drown.

No matter what anyone will say,
I tried so hard and at the end of the day,
I gave my best and did all I could,
nothing else to do that I should.

Didn't think I'd lose this race
and end up here in last place,
but life goes on and so does love,
I'll trust in divine guidance from above.

# I Hate Sleeping Alone

I lay alone in the expanse of the bed
and hug the pillow to the side of my head,
too many long weeks you've been gone
and I hate sleeping alone…

Your brief returns were a bliss-filled time,
we'd both push each other, higher each climb,
then you'd leave, sadness filled my soul,
and I hate sleeping alone…

At first each other, we dearly missed,
then at some point we both got pissed,
this boat has sailed so far off course, and oh —
and I hate sleeping alone….

I miss you reaching out for me,
pulling me flush into your body,
lips on my neck, my body you owned —
and I hate sleeping alone…

Your scent, it barely lingers here,
been so long since you've whispered in my ear,
our love has dried up, now where do we go?
'Cause I hate sleeping alone…

Now sex only serves to scratch an itch,
Mistress Life is a cruel, cruel, bitch.
How much longer can this go on?
'Cause I hate sleeping alone…

The sex is still good,
but I wish you would
look at me the way you used to,
my heart and soul ache for you.
How am I supposed to go on,
when I hate sleeping alone?

# Waiting

Like looking through a dirty window
I squint, and clean the glass;
still I can't see you, but
I know you're out there somewhere.

One day, you will appear
when I least expect it;
you'll stand right in front of me
and I'll recognize you.

Your eyes will connect with mine,
your mouth will turn up at the corners
the same as me,
and we'll know…we'll know…

You'll take my hand,
my fingers will curl around yours
and clasp tightly,
as if we've always done so.

When you lower your face to mine
and whisper those words
meant only for me,
my heart will beat in time with yours.

Your lips will touch mine
like we've done it a thousand times;
there will be sparks, and softness
the way it should be.

You will enfold me in your arms
and I'll fit, like I was made for you;
our bodies will join
and it will be new…and yet familiar.

But now you're the light
at the end of my tunnel,
softly glowing, waiting
for me to find you at the end.

*Surrender*
*Pain*
*Need*
*Love*
*Unconditional*
*Surrender*

# Desires

# Of

# The

# Heart

*Lust*
*Violent*
*Passion*
*Taken*
*Given*
*Possession*
*Mine*

# Dreaming of Him

When sundown ends daylight
and I slip under the sheets at night,
thoughts of you constantly run through my head
and I imagine you here in my bed.

Our naked bodies stretched out side by side
bodies are hot, our fingers entwined,
we look deeply into each other's eyes
and I tell you, "you're mine..."

Your rock-hard length presses into me;
I sling a leg over your hip, trying to take you in deeply;
you chuckle, telling me, "We have all night…"
And here in my mind, I know you are right

Rubbing your shaft through my slick pussy
making me feel like a wanton hussy;
the feel of your lips on mine,
dancing fingertips over my skin,
everything so right, it is like manna from heaven.

Passion consumes and we fully embrace,
wrapped around each other, I love your taste;
your lips travel down my neck to my nipple
close your mouth over, through my body ecstasy ripples.

My hand skims down your side, grasping your ass
you nip at my bud, and I can't help but gasp.
The air heats around us and we rock 'gainst each other,
desire is fueled and this can only be sated together

You roll me to my back and settle between my thighs;
I breathe your scent in deeply and sigh,
your hardness pulsing against my swollen folds,
your hard body on top of me is a sight to behold.

Legs spread wide, you slide to the hilt as I invite you in,
your thickness filling me, I shift before we begin.
Long smooth strokes inside my tight channel,
stoke up the fire
you caress my face, kiss my breast,
as we both rise higher

Hips pumping rhythmically, my hands take in the
smooth skin of your back,
and I can't help but to thrust back,
sucking the sweat from your neck,
gripping your shoulders, nails biting into your skin
being here, making love to you — this must be heaven

I roll you to your back and ride you with ease,
the glide of your cock in my wet,
hot pussy, such a tease.
Thrusting upward, bouncing me, you call my name,
shape my breasts in your hands, feels so right,
we carry no shame

Rising up to meet me, you flip me to my knees,
holding me captive to do as you please,
one arm round my waist, one fist in my hair
thrust in from behind, how far do we dare?

I collapse, and you pin me to the bed;
your breath in my ear makes lust spin my head
pumping so hard, I take it — it's all I can do
like no other pleasure, this connection with you.

You withdraw and turn me so we're face to face,
it's the homestretch now to finish this race;
our hands clasped tightly over my head
you drive me straight into the bed.

Eyes locked on each other, no need for words,
unspoken understanding, doesn't need to be heard;
with one final thrust I tumble over the edge
with a growl, I know you teeter on the ledge,
wrap my legs 'round your waist I cry out,
then you throw your head back and shout.

Your name a repeated whisper on my lips,
as your weight settles in the cradle of my hips;
my eyes close, stroke my fingers through your hair
to stay like this — the world forgotten without care,
feel your limbs shake, as you crush the breath out of me,
breathe in your scent, open my eyes to see.

Reality crashes down, I'm alone and flushed,
tears fill my eyes, feeling somewhat crushed;
roll to the side, hug my pillow to my breast
longing to quell the ache in my chest,
I sigh, let the tears roll down my cheeks
dreaming of you, I drift off to sleep…

# Flash in the Dark

Lightning flashes, thunder rolls, I wake with a start
clutching a hand over my rapidly beating heart;
a storm rages outside, and I'm breathing fast
another crash startles — how long this will last?

Your hand on my shoulder reassures me anew,
and I relax back into the warmth that is you,
nuzzling my neck, whispering so I can hear
words of tenderness, passion and love in my ear.

Hot breath tickles, a shiver runs down my spine,
you chuckle, staking your claim, "You're mine…"
shuddering as your fingertips dance across my skin
and feelings of love replace the fear within.

Down the side of my neck you brush a soft kiss,
I melt into your arms in such utter bliss,
you enfold me in the warmth of your embrace,
and I turn my head so we're face to face.

Your mouth captures mine with fierce passion,
wet heat invades, and after a fashion,
you lower me slowly back onto the bed,
a hand guiding, cradling the back of my head.

Tugging my nipple between your teeth,
quick pain followed by warm, wet relief,
I arch into you as my breath hisses out,
tongue curls 'round my nipple, makes me shout.

You journey down lower, taking a trip south
fingers graze your head as you open your hot mouth,
a shiver runs through me from head to toe,
feel you smile 'gainst my skin, the first flick so slow.

Exploring my folds at an unhurried pace,
but never staying long enough in one place,
hips writhing and wriggling underneath you,
moaning out my pleasure is all I can do.

I beg you to slide your cock into me,
you hold me captive, I've no wish to be free,
head thrashes side to side, tongue flicking quickly,
bringing me right…to the very edge of ecstasy.

Your name is now a chant on my lips,
your hands bite my flesh, pinning down my hips,
long, leisurely licks slow down the ride,
groan in agony, my longing, I can't hide.

Lightning strikes; illuminating the room,
thunder resounds as the orgasm blooms,
deep in my core it begins like a wave,
exploding like dynamite from my woman's cave.

My body tenses, then shakes like a leaf,
a soft kiss to my temple is the only relief
you offer as you rise up over top of me,
first probing, then thrusting your cock into me.

Driving into my sheath with relentless speed
creating a torturous, mindless need,
my nails bite your flesh as my fingers grasp,
each of my breaths come out as a gasp.

You roll us to the side, your lips search out mine,
you continue to thrust as our tongues entwine,
my arms wrap around your broad back,
with you here, heaven is found in the pitch black.

Lightning strikes once more, makes your eyes shine,
I see to your soul and know you're truly mine,
your shaft glides easily through my woman's dew,
further awakening my desire for you.

One last thrust you bury your cock deep,
I cry out, the pleasure making me weep,
your hot cum spurts inside of me,
I cling to you, love being joined to your body.

You whisper the words I need to hear
as you stroke some hair back behind my ear,
I bury my head under your chin,
hugging you, keeping you deep within.

Rain pelts the window, my breath hot on your chest,
my heart beating a staccato 'gainst my breast,
bodies entwined, we stay as we are,
breathing slows, knowing sleep isn't far.

Drop a kiss to my hair, love spears my heart,
secure in your arms, never want to be apart,
your love makes me feel safe and whole,
you are the one who completes my soul.

# I Watch

I watch
as you enter the room,
tired from your long day
you don't see me.

Stretching arms overhead,
you lift your hair and
it cascades down your back.

Cock stiffens—
I take hold, eyes greedy
as you unbutton your blouse,
mulling over your day.
You kick off your heels,
your shirt flutters to the floor,
you reach behind,
undo the clasp of your bra.

I lean forward,
heart rate quickens,
your nipples exposed, pucker
as you toss the lace to the bed.

My gaze sharpens
like a cat in the dark
ready to pounce,
but I keep to the shadows,
not ready yet to make
my presence known.

You caress one breast,
pluck your nipple, a sigh.
Are you wet like I want you to be?
Are you thinking of me? Waiting for me?

I ease lower in the chair
to lessen my ache, balls full
my hunger for you raging.

You drop your skirt
wriggle out of your pantyhose;
lust clogs my lungs,
the movement of your ass,
long to squeeze it in my grasp,
makes me harder,
the lace around your hips,
I want to tear off with my teeth,
plunge into you, take you,
make you scream when,
we cum together.

A groan escapes—
slowly, you turn
make out my shadow in the corner.

I see your provocative smile,
the way one hand skims
down your belly, dips into your panties.

My breathing ceases,
your hand disappears, reappears
glistening with your dew.

You wet your lip,
bring your finger to your mouth,
tasting what I crave.

I tense, ready to leap;
you stop me with one raised finger;
I relax back, cock hard,
ready for your wet heat.

A slick sheet of sweat covers my body,
my swollen head leaks
for wanting you.
I stroke.

One shake of your head
and I grip the arms of the chair,
eager to do your bidding.

My muscles shake as
you stroll over,
sliding the lace down your hips;
stepping out of it
as you sashay toward me.

Toes grip the carpet,
your arousal invades my senses,
my head spins
as you climb onto my lap;
poised over my cock
nectar dripping from your core, curls damp
nails biting into my shoulders.

I wait
and watch.

# Touch Me

Kiss me on the cheek,
haven't seen you in a week,
thoughts go through my head,
I just want you in my bed,
my fantasy's areelin'
oh, I just have this feelin',
there's no need to hide,
come on, take me for a ride.

Do we have a half an hour?
I want to love you in the shower,
only you I want to please,
even get down on my knees.
I'm your dirty little girl,
come on, let's give it a whirl,
let's take a trip down south,
gonna put you in my mouth.

So, touch me, hold me.
Kiss me, scold me.
Baby, lock the door,
we'll just do it on the floor

So, touch me, hold me.
Kiss me, scold me.
You know I just can't fake it;
I just wanna see you naked…


I'm your sexy little lady;
now I've been thinkin' maybe,
let's do it all night long;
feels so good it can't be wrong.
Let's do it on the table.
Hell — I'm willing and I'm able.
You've no need for the rest,
'cause you know I am the best.


I see you wet your lips,
you know I can't resist,
just want a little taste,
so there's no time to waste.
You know I like it rough,
I just can't get enough,
not feelin' no shame
when I'm screaming out your name!

So, touch me, hold me.
Kiss me, scold me.
Baby, lock the door;
we'll just do it on the floor.
So, touch me, hold me.
Kiss me, scold me.
You know I just can't fake it;
I just wanna see you naked…

# Making Up

Hanging my head in shame and despair,
at times, life seems so bloody unfair,
then I feel your arms come around me
and I relax back into your solid body.

Your warmth and strength bring me relief,
dispelling my earlier anger and grief,
tipping my face up to yours, and then I see
your eyes provide a promise and an apology.

Nipples pucker and I firmly grip your arms,
as you seduce me using all of your charms,
"Hush", you say, as your lips descend toward mine,
our tongues tangle in a dance as old as time.

The hard swell of your thick cock against my back,
for making me so hot, you have such a knack,
my longing for you wells up like a wave inside
I moan loudly, my yearning for you I cannot hide.

Our dumb fight made me feel like such a prick,
you oblige, slipping your hand down to my dick,
one of your hands brush over my chest,
hard, I shift in my seat, needy for the rest.

All is now forgotten with your first caress,
one word I groan over and over — "Yes, yes…"
pumping my steel shaft up into your hand,
"Get up", you chuckle, and then tell me to stand.

You hold me so tight, I cannot escape,
hot lips brand my skin; your teeth bite my nape,
fingers thread through my hair, pulling, then hard clasp,
my nails scrape the skin of your thighs as I gasp.

Your firm grip stroking my cock so ruthlessly,
easily you bring me to mindless ecstasy,
hot breath in my ear, my world is turned inside out,
balls tighten; I come with one glorious shout.

Your fingertips brushing over my member,
soft kisses, tongue flicks out, your love so tender,
"Come to bed now, baby", to me you whisper,
supporting me, I follow you with a whimper.

Down onto the bed we tumble together,
my only wish is to stay in your arms forever,
wrapping our limbs around each other so tight,
one stellar moment of bliss, makes the world right.

# And Then There Were Three

With a giggle she pulled me into the room,
I blinked and shivered in the dusty gloom,
"I've never done this before," I whispered,
"Relax," she offered, tipping my face up, I kissed her.

She palms my breast, her hand skims down my side,
breathing quickens, need rises, desire I cannot hide,
her lips so soft, I twine my fingers through her hair,
lost in this moment, I didn't sense he was there.

A throat clears, we jump and make out eyes
gleaming in the dark,
gliding silently across the room, he says,
"Come here for a lark?"
He brushes aside the hair from my neck,
cornering me in,
"So pretty," he breathes, and I slowly turn to face him.

A lustful gleam in his eye, he grins, his fangs protrude,
"Forgive me ladies — I don't mean to be rude,
You both seem to be having so much fun,
Won't you let me join your one-on-one?"

"I don't know," I respond with a spine tingling shiver,
"Let's go for it," my sexy cohort delivers.
To my surprise, she clasps my hands behind my back,
an adventuresome nature, she has a knack.
I shrink back, but she hisses, "Let him have his way."
Being held captive now, I really have no say,
he leans in to inhale my scent, fear mixes with need,
his lips brush my neck, I pay the warning no heed.

The heat from his hand hovers over my breast,
"May I?" he asks, I nod, wanting the rest.
"So firm and round," he murmurs, suckling the peak,
I arch into his mouth, my legs going weak.

His hand slides down my stomach, cupping my mound,
one finger finds my clit, and it circles around,
"That's it," she encourages, her tongue flicks my ear,
blood rushing through my veins is all I can hear.

Her hand squeezes my tit, he kicks my stance wide,
showing me no mercy, there's nowhere to hide,
with one finger, he pierces my core,
stroking the fire, all I want is more.

Overwhelmed, the orgasm washes through me,
shaking and quivering, I can hardly breathe.
He smiles, "Come my pet, we have all night."
Stunned, I follow him, further away from the light.

She trails behind us, caressing my hair,
I shiver as he leads me further into his lair,
He shrugs out of his clothes, stroking his length
"Next ladies? In spades, I have strength."

# *END*

# About the Author

Kellie is a PRO member of the Romance Writers of America, and a contributing blogger for the Ass Cheek Angels and The Naughty Romance Writers. As a former elite gymnast and coach, she loves to base stories around the sport she's been involved with for most of her life. Her sensual novel and short story writing allows her to spread her vivid imagination to everyone out there willing to listen. She writes seductive tales where characters come to life and touch your heart and soul, making your fingers tingle with anticipation. Of course it goes without saying, you might find a special surprise when each word you read pleases your every desire...

You can visit her at:

www.kelliekamryn.com

or drop by her blog at

www.kelliekamryn.blogspot.com

# Also by Kellie Kamryn
# From
# Romance Divine LLC

## *Going for Gold*

It was an office Christmas party filled with sexual tension. Gymnastics coach Grant Howard couldn't keep his eyes off the newly-hired cheerleader coach. And sultry Teena Adams felt the same way about him. The "rah-rah-rahs" she felt were cheers of unbridled lust. From punch and cookies to sexual escapades on gym apparatus, you'll never look at Christmas parties or a trampoline the same way again. It's winner-take-all, when lovers are *Going for Gold*.

## *Secrets and Desires of the Heart*

Watch for the e-book, and the audio version read by Kellie Kamryn, coming in 2012.

Also Available From Romance Divine LLC at:
www.romancedivine.com
and
Other fine e-book and print book retailers.

## Contemporary Romance

### From Andrea Glenn
*Safe Haven*
*Miami Desire*
*The Coffee Shop*
*Style of a Lifetime*

### From Bryn Colvin
*Late Night Sessions* (Also in print)

### From Ronna Gage
*Bare It All*
*Love Lessons*

### From Jodi Olson
*Getting Wild*
*Playing House*
*Storm's Obsession*
*Breathless Whispers*
*Seduction - The Riley Way*

### From Carol Cassada
*Going Home Again*

### From Elizabeth Black
*Indiscretions Vol. I*
*Indiscretions Vol. II*

From Mary Suzanne
*Jade*
*Addie*
*Loving Katie*
*Darling Rebel*
*Spanish Rose*
*Rekindled Love*
*Chance Encounter*
*Mistaken Identity*

## Older Women and Younger Men

From J.A. Rawls
*3-Way Weekend*
*Cougar Bounty*
*Cougar Awakening*

From Jodi Olson
*Sinful Delights*
*Christmas in Cuffs*

From Elizabeth Black
*Indiscretions Vol. I*

## Holiday Romance

From Bryn Colvin
*Rekindling the Belfire*

From J.A. Rawls
*Elf at Play*
*Christmas Creep*
*All I Want For Christmas*

# Contemporary Christian

## From Deborah A. Hodge
*The Calling* (Also in print)
*The Witness* (Also in print)

# Multiple-Partner and Threesomes

## From Jodi Olson
*Dear John*
*Claiming Lauren*
*Raining on Sunday*
*Naughty Whispers*
*Christmas in Cuffs*
*Hunter's Possession*
*Fir the Love of Bobbie*
*Sensuous Pleasures (Print)*
*Tempting Pleasures (Print)*

## From J.A. Rawls
*Nation's Call*
*BJ's Cowboys*
*Angel's Delight*
*3-Way Weekend*
*Play It Again Sam*

## From Ronna Gage
*Friends and Lovers*

## From Elizabeth Black
*Feral Heat*
*Indiscretions Vol. II*

From Mary Suzanne
*Drifter*
*My Cowboys*
*Sexual Knead*
*Fantasy Games*
*Sexy Hitchhikers*
*Double Your Pleasure*

From Jennifer Labelle
*Naughty Noel*
*Leather and Pleasure*
*Sinfully Sexy: Leather and Pleasure 3*

## Action and Adventure

From Gregory Causey
*Hitler's Will* (Also in print)
From Bailey Griffin
*Simply Suitable*
*Perfectly Proper*

## Paranormal

From Andrea Glenn
*A Dark Night in Paris*

From Elizabeth Black
*Feral Heat*
*Fountain of Youth*

# Male-Male and Lesbian

### From Elizabeth Black
*Feral Heat*
*Indiscretions Vol. II*

### From Mary Suzanne
*Secrets*
*Triangle*
*Partners*
*Marooned*
*Love Train*
*Love Cruise*
*Angel In Blue*
*Sexual Knead*
*Private Dancer*
*Sexy Hitchhikers*
*Fantasy Games*
*Just Not Into Me*
*A New Beginning*
*More Than Friends*

### From J.A. Rawls
*Man-Oh-Man*

### From Constance Pennington Smythe
*Corporate Slaves: The Men - One: Hostile Takeover*
*Corporate Slaves: The Men - Two: Office Rituals*
*Corporate Slaves: The Women - One: Recruitment*

### From Jennifer Labelle
*Naughty Noel*
*Leather and Pleasure*
*Sinfully Sexy: Leather and Pleasure 3*

From Jodi Olson
*Dear John*
*For the Love of Bobbie*

## Print Romance Anthologies

From Mary Suzanne
*SEXY: Mary Suzanne's Erotic Romance Collection*

From Jodi Olson
*Tempting Pleasures*
*Sensuous Pleasures*

## Aviation Art

From Danny Causey and Gregory Causey
*Denizens of the Desert*
(Print: Photographs by Danny Causey;
Edited by Greg Causey)

## Poetry

From Sarah J. Head
*At Home and Away*
(Available as e-book, print and audio book)

## BDSM/Fetish/Chastity/Cuckold

From Elizabeth Black
*Feral Heat*

## From Jennifer Labelle
*Naughty Noel*
*Leather and Pleasure*
*Sinfully Sexy: Leather and Pleasure 3*
*When Sparks Ignite: Leather and Pleasure 2*

## From Constance Pennington Smythe
*Mistress Karin*
*The Breaking Cage*
*Female Domination: Short Stories - Vol. I*
*Corporate Slaves: The Men - One: Hostile Takeover*
*Corporate Slaves: The Men - Two: Office Rituals*
*Corporate Slaves: The Women - One: Recruitment*
<u>*The Chastity Cuckold Tales Series*</u>
*WSB Club*
*Black Owned*
*Family Cuckold*
*The Conversation*
*Cuckold Panty Wall*
*Cuckold Fluffer Box*
*My Daddy Does Your Wife*

# Ballroom Dance

## From Gregory Causey and Natasha Yushanov
*Dancing With Natasha* (Also in Print)